Indonesia

Sue Townsend and Caroline Young

Heinemann Library
Chicago, Illinois

© 2003 Heinemann Library
a division of Reed Elsevier Inc.
Chicago, Illinois

Customer Service 888-454-2279

Visit our website at
www.heinemannlibrary.com

Designed by Jo Hinton-Malivoire and
Tinstar Design Limited (www.tinstar.co.uk)
Illustrations by Nicholas Beresford-Davies
Originated by Dot Gradations Ltd
Printed in China
by Wing King Tong

07 06 05 04 03
10 9 8 7 6 5 4 3 2 1

**Library of Congress Cataloging-in-
Publication Data**
Townsend, Sue, 1963-
  Indonesia / Sue Townsend & Caroline Young.
    p. cm. -- (A world of recipes)
Summary: Presents recipes from Indonesia that
reflect the ingredients and culture of the
country.
Includes bibliographical references and index.
 ISBN 1-4034-0976-5
 1. Cookery, Indonesian--Juvenile literature.
[1. Cookery, Indonesian.
2. Food habits--Indonesia.] I. Young, Caroline,
1939- II. Title.
 TX724.5.I5T69 2003
 641.59598--dc21

2002155858

Acknowledgments
The author and publishers are grateful to the
following for permission to reproduce
copyright material: p. 5 Corbis; all other
photographs Gareth Boden.

Cover photographs reproduced with
permission of Gareth Boden.

The publishers would like to thank Diyan
Paratihani for her assistance with the
preparation of this book.

Every effort has been made to contact
copyright holders of any material reproduced
in this book. Any omissions will be rectified in
subsequent printings if notice is given to the
publisher.

Some words are shown in
bold, **like this.** You can find
out what they mean by
looking in the glossary.

Contents

Key

* easy

** medium

*** difficult

Indonesian Food

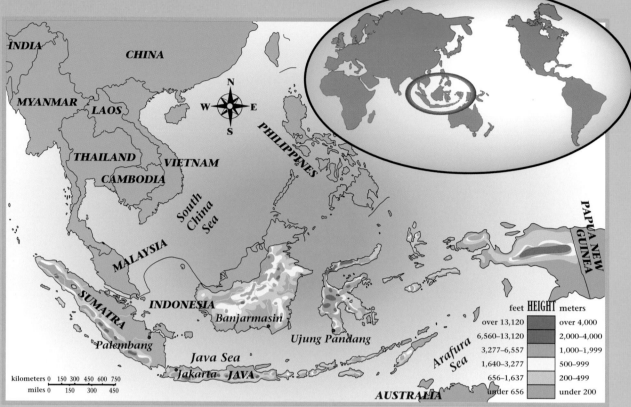

Indonesia is in southeast Asia. It is made up of more than 17,000 islands, but people only live on 6,000 of them. This chain of islands is called an **archipelago**, and it stretches across the ocean between Malaysia to the northwest and Australia to the southeast.

In the past

Throughout the centuries, many different people have visited the islands of Indonesia. Sailors from Malaysia left the mainland in small boats and landed there more than 4,000 years ago. Traders from China, India, and Arabia settled there, bringing their customs and cooking styles. In 1602, traders from the Netherlands took control of the islands, naming them the Dutch East Indies. They took over all farming, including growing spices such as nutmeg, cloves, and peppers—the islands' most important trade. Most of Indonesia became independent in 1949. Today, many people live in Indonesia's busy cities, but in the countryside, people live in a more traditional way.

Around the country

It is hot nearly year-round in Indonesia. The main difference in the weather from place to place is how much rain falls. In many

Rice is the most important crop in Indonesia. The rice grows in flooded paddy fields, but before harvesting, the fields are drained.

areas, the **monsoon** wind from China brings very heavy rain from December to March. From June to September, a dry wind from Australia blows across the islands, and little rain falls. High mountain ranges, with volcanoes and rain forests, cover many of the islands.

Rice is Indonesia's most important crop. In Java, farmers can grow two or three crops of rice a year. On Java and on other islands further east, farmers grow coconuts, palm oil trees, or tobacco on large **plantations**. Fishing is very important for people living on Indonesia's long coastline.

Indonesian meals

Indonesian meals are usually made up of several dishes laid out on the table at the same time. People take a spoonful of rice, then choose some of the other dishes. Food is often hot and spicy, with cilantro, pepper, and garlic the most important flavors.

5

Ingredients

pineapple

mango

ginger

bean sprouts

coconut milk

lemongrass

chili peppers

ginger

peanuts

cilantro leaves

shrimp paste

Bean sprouts

Bean sprouts grow from mung beans. You can buy them at grocery stores or farmer's markets. Always buy bean sprouts that look fresh and crisp.

Candlenuts

Candlenuts look like large, pale hazelnuts. They make people sick if eaten raw, so they are **ground** up and added to sauces. If you cannot find them, use Brazil nuts.

Chili Peppers

Indonesian recipes often contain chili peppers. If you don't like spicy food, add less pepper than suggested, or leave it out. Most grocery stores sell chili peppers fresh, **chopped**, packed in jars, or dried. Be sure to use chili peppers, not bird's eye chilies. Throw away the seeds, and wash your hands thoroughly after touching them— chili pepper juice can irritate your eyes and skin.

6

Cilantro

The leaves, root, and seeds of the cilantro herb are used to flavor many Indonesian dishes. Each part of the cilantro plant has a slightly different flavor.

Coconut milk

Coconut milk is made from coconut flesh, not the liquid inside a fresh coconut. You can buy coconut milk in cans, or as a powder.

Fresh ginger

Fresh ginger is a root, which is **peeled** and **grated.** It adds a warm, slightly lemony flavor to dishes. Most grocery stores sell it. You cannot use dried, ground ginger for the recipes in this book.

Lemongrass

Lemongrass has a delicate, lemony flavor. Indonesian cooks use it to flavor many dishes.

Palm sugar

This sugar is made from the juice of the coconut palm flower. It is dark brown and very hard. Use dark brown sugar if you cannot find palm sugar.

Peanuts

Peanuts are also called groundnuts. Indonesian cooks use them to flavor foods and thicken sauces. Use peanuts that have not been **roasted**, unless the recipe says otherwise.

Shrimp paste

This strongly flavored paste is made from crushed shrimp, and is very salty. If you cannot find it, use anchovy essence instead.

Before You Start

Kitchen rules

There are a few basic rules you should always follow when you are cooking:

- Ask an adult if you can use the kitchen.
- Some cooking processes, especially those involving hot water or oil, can be dangerous. When you see this sign, take extra care or ask an adult to help.
- Wash your hands before you start.
- Wear an apron to protect your clothes.
- Be very careful when you use sharp knives.
- Never leave pan handles sticking out because you might bump into them and spill hot food.
- Use oven mitts to lift things in and out of the oven.
- Wash fruits and vegetables before you use them.
- Always wash chopping boards very well after use, especially after chopping raw meat, fish, or poultry.
- Use a separate chopping board for onions and garlic, if possible.

How long will it take?

Some of the recipes in this book are quick and easy, and some are more difficult and take longer. The stripe across the right-hand side of each recipe page tells you how long it takes to prepare a dish from start to finish. It also shows how difficult each recipe is to make: * (easy), ** (medium), or *** (difficult).

Quantities and measurements

You can see how many people each recipe will serve at the top of each right-hand page. You can multiply or divide the quantities if you want to cook for more or fewer people.

Ingredients for recipes can be measured in two ways. Imperial measurements use cups and ounces. Metric measurements use grams and milliliters.

In the recipes, you will see the following abbreviations:

tbsp = tablespoon	oz = ounce	cm = centimeter
tsp = teaspoon	lb = pound	g = gram
ml = milliliter	in. = inch	

Utensils

To cook the recipes in this book, you will need these utensils (as well as essentials, such as spoons, plates, and bowls):

- plastic or glass chopping board (easier to clean than wooden ones)
- food processor or blender
- large frying pan
- 10-in. (25-cm) heavy-based non-stick frying pan
- lemon squeezer
- measuring cup
- wok or large saucepan with lid
- small saucepan with lid
- sieve
- set of scales
- grater
- sharp knife
- palette knife
- baking sheets
- steamer or metal colander
- wooden **skewers**

(!) Whenever you use kitchen knives, be very careful.

Peanut Fritters

In Indonesia, street vendors sell these fritters as take-out food. They are called *rempeyk kacang* (pronounced *rum-PAY-ek-kah-chang*). You can serve them on their own as a snack, or with other dishes as part of a meal.

What you need

1 clove garlic
2 oz (50 g) **roasted** salted peanuts
2 oz (50 g) rice flour
½ tsp **ground** coriander
½ tsp ground cumin
½ tsp ground turmeric
½ tsp baking powder
6 tbsp coconut milk
1 tbsp groundnut or vegetable oil
9 tbsp water

What you do

1 **Peel** and finely **chop** or crush the garlic.

2 Put the peanuts into a blender, and **blend** briefly until roughly chopped.

3 Put the garlic, peanuts, rice flour, coriander, cumin, turmeric, and baking powder into a bowl.

4 Stir the coconut milk and 9 tbsp water together in a bowl. Add the liquid to the peanut mixture.

(!) 5 Heat the oil in a large frying pan over medium heat. Put 1 tbsp of peanut mixture into the pan.

6 Add three or four more fritters to the pan, leaving a space between then. **Fry** for 2 minutes, until the mixture looks set.

7 Use a palette knife or a spatula to turn the fritters over, and cook for another 2 minutes, until they are golden brown.

8 Lift the cooked fritters onto a paper towel to **drain** while you cook the rest of the mixture. Serve the fritters hot or cold.

GROUNDNUT OIL
Many Indonesian dishes are cooked in groundnut oil, which is made from peanuts. If you cannot find groundnut oil, use vegetable oil instead.

Peanut Sauce

Indonesian people often serve spicy sauces, called *sambals*, with their meals. Try serving this peanut sauce with Chicken Satay (page 22) or with Vegetable Gado-Gado (page 14). You can keep it in a container in the refrigerator for up to three days.

What you need

1 clove garlic
1 small onion
½ red chili pepper (if you like it)
14 oz (400 g) raw peanuts (not **roasted**) in their shells or 7 oz (200 g) shelled raw peanuts
4 tbsp vegetable or groundnut oil
1 tsp shrimp paste or anchovy essence
1 tsp palm sugar or brown sugar
1 tbsp dark soy sauce
1 cup (240 ml) water

What you do

1 **Peel** the garlic and onion, and **chop** them finely.

2 Cut the piece of chili pepper in half and throw away the seeds. Chop the pepper finely. Wash your hands well afterwards.

3 Take the peanuts out of their shells, if necessary.

⚠ 4 Heat the oil in a wok over medium heat. Add the peanuts and cook for 3–4 minutes, stirring all the time. Turn the heat off.

5 Using a slotted spoon, lift the peanuts into a bowl, leaving the oil in the wok.

(!) **6** Heat the wok again over medium heat, and **fry** the garlic, onion and pepper for 1 minute. Turn the heat off, and spoon them into the bowl with the peanuts.

7 Put the peanuts and onion mixture into a blender, and **blend** until smooth. Empty the mixture into a saucepan.

8 Stir the shrimp paste, sugar, soy sauce, and 1 cup (240 ml) of water into the peanut mixture. Cook over a low heat, stirring all the time, until it is **simmering.** Simmer for 3 minutes, then serve.

Vegetable Gado-Gado

This dish is a favorite in Indonesian restaurants around the world. In Indonesia, street vendors sell it wrapped in banana leaves as a snack. Serve it with Peanut Sauce (page 12).

What you need

6 medium-sized potatoes
Pinch of salt
4 eggs
Half a cucumber
1 cup (100 g) spinach
1 cup (100 g) white cabbage
1 cup (100 g) bean sprouts
1 cup (100 g) tofu
2 tbsp groundnut or vegetable oil
2-oz (50-g) packet ready-cooked prawn crackers

What you do

(!) **1 Peel** the potatoes. Put them in a pan with a pinch of salt. Cover them with **boiling** water, and cook for 20 minutes. When cooked, **drain** them, and cover them with cold water.

2 Put the eggs into a pan, cover with boiling water, and **simmer** for 8 minutes. Place eggs into a bowl of cold water.

3 Cut cucumber into ½-in. (1-cm) slices, then cut into fours. Put them into a sieve, sprinkle with salt, and leave the sieve over a bowl.

4 Wash the spinach and pat it dry. Finely **shred** the spinach and white cabbage.

(!) **5** Pour boiling water into a large saucepan. Add the cabbage and bring back to a boil. Add the spinach and bean sprouts, and drain immediately.

6 Cover the vegetables with cold water, then drain again.

⚠ **7** Cut the tofu into ½-in. (1-cm) cubes. Heat the oil in a frying pan or wok, and **fry** the tofu for 2–3 minutes. Carefully lift the tofu onto paper towels.

8 Peel the shells off the eggs. Cut them into quarters.

9 Rinse the cucumber wedges and leave them to drain.

10 Cut the potatoes into 1-in. (2½-cm) cubes.

11 Arrange all the ingredients on a plate. Serve with prawn crackers and Peanut Sauce (page 12).

Crab and Baby Sweet Corn Soup

In Indonesia, people serve soup with all their other dishes. If the other food on the table is spicy, the soup is made milder to balance the flavors.

What you need

6 green onions

7 oz (200 g) baby sweet corn

1-in. (2½-cm) piece fresh ginger

4 oz (100 g) tofu

1 tbsp groundnut or vegetable oil

Pinch of chili pepper powder (if you like it)

1 chicken stock cube

1 tbsp granulated sugar

1 tbsp light soy sauce

6 oz (170 g) can white crab meat

3 tbsp fresh cilantro

2½ cups (600 ml) water

What you do

1 Trim both ends from the green onions. Finely **slice** the white and green parts of the onion, and keep separate.

2 Cut the baby sweet corn into ½-in. (1-cm) pieces. **Peel** the ginger and cut it into 3 slices.

3 Cut the tofu into ½-in. (1-cm) cubes.

4 Heat the oil in a saucepan over medium heat. **Fry** the white part of the green onions for 2 minutes. Add the sweet corn, ginger, tofu, and chili pepper powder, and cook for 2 minutes, stirring all the time.

(!) 5 Lift the tofu out onto paper towels.
Crumble the stock cube and add to the pan
with the sugar, soy sauce, and 2½ cups (600 ml)
hot water. **Cover** and **simmer** for 15 minutes.

6 Using a slotted spoon, lift out the pieces of
ginger, and throw them away.

7 Add the crab meat, tofu, and green onion tops.
Cook for 3 minutes.

8 **Chop** the cilantro and stir into the soup. Serve
immediately.

Prawn and Ric Noodl Sou

This filling soup is made with meat, vegetables, and thin noodles made from rice flour, called *miehun* (pronounced *mee-hoon*) in Indonesia.

What you need

1 chicken breast
5 green onions
1 clove garlic
2-in. (5-cm) piece fresh
  ginger
1 chicken stock cube
1 tbsp groundnut or
  vegetable oil
1 tsp **ground** coriander
¼ tsp ground turmeric
6 oz (170 g) rice noodles
1¼ cup (300 ml) coconut
  milk
3 oz (75 g) bean sprouts
5 oz (150 g) peeled prawns
2 cups (500 ml) water

What you do

① **1** Put the chicken into a pan and cover it with water. **Cover** the pan, bring the water to a **boil**, and **simmer** for 20 minutes.

2 Meanwhile, trim both ends off the green onions. Finely **slice** the white and green parts, keeping them separate.

3 **Peel** the garlic and crush, or finely **chop**, it.

4 Peel and finely **grate** the ginger.

5 Using a slotted spoon, lift the chicken breast onto a board to cool. Keep the cooking liquid.

6 Cut the cooked chicken into thin slices. Crumble the stock cube into a measuring cup. Add chicken liquid and water to make 2 cups (500 ml).

① **7** Heat the oil in a wok or saucepan. **Stir-fry** the white part of the spring onions for 1 minute. Add the garlic, ginger, coriander, and turmeric, and stir-fry for 30 seconds.

8 Add the chicken, and stir-fry for 1 minute. Pour in the stock and bring the soup to a boil. Cover and simmer for 20 minutes.

(!) **9** Put the noodles into a pan of boiling water for 5 minutes, then **drain** them.

10 Stir in the noodles and coconut milk. Add the bean sprouts, prawns, and green onion tops. Simmer for 3 minutes and serve.

Nasi Goreng

In Indonesia, this dish of fried rice, chicken, beef, and prawns is often served **garnished** with onion rings and strips of omelette as a delicious meal.

What you need

10 oz (300 g) basmati rice or fragrant Thai rice
1 chicken breast
7 oz (200 g) beef fillet
1–2 fresh red chili peppers (if you like them)
2 cloves garlic
1 onion
2 tbsp groundnut or vegetable oil
4 oz (100 g) peeled prawns
2 tbsp dark soy sauce
1 tsp shrimp paste or anchovy essence
2½ cups (600 ml) water

To garnish:
For omelette strips:
2 eggs
Salt and pepper
1 tbsp groundnut or vegetable oil

For crispy onion rings:
1 onion
2 tbsp groundnut or vegetable oil

What you do

(!) 1 Put the rice in a pan with 2½ cups (600 ml) **boiling** water. Bring to a boil and **simmer** for 20 minutes.

2 **Drain** the rice in a colander. Put it over a bowl and run cold water over the rice.

(!) 3 Put the chicken breast into a small pan. **Cover** with water and bring it to a boil. Cover and simmer for 20 minutes.

4 Make the omelette strips (see 6–8 on page 39) and crispy onion rings (page 25).

5 Lift the chicken onto a board to cool, then cut it into thin strips.

6 Cut the beef fillet into thin slices.

7 Cut the chili peppers in half and throw away seeds. **Chop** the pepper finely, then wash your hands.

8 **Peel** and chop, or crush, the garlic. Peel and **slice** the onion into rings.

9 Put the onion, chili pepper, and garlic into a blender, and **blend** until smooth.

(!) 10 Heat the oil in a wok and **fry** the blended mixture for 1 minute. Add the beef and **stir-fry** for 2 minutes. Add the prawns and chicken, and stir-fry for another 2 minutes.

11 Add the rice, soy sauce, and shrimp paste. Cook for 5 minutes.

12 Spoon the mixture onto a serving plate. Serve, garnished with omelette strips and onion rings.

Chicken Satay

Indonesian cooks make *satay*, which is **marinated** meat on a stick. Street vendors sell *satay* as a snack, and people buy it to eat as part of a main meal. Serve it with Peanut Sauce (page 12).

What you need

1 onion
2 cloves garlic
2 candlenuts or
   Brazil nuts
1 stem lemongrass
½ tsp chili pepper
   powder (if you like it)
1 tsp **ground** coriander
1 tsp ground cumin
Pinch of ground cloves
1 tsp ground cinnamon
½ tsp ground nutmeg
½ tsp ground turmeric
2 tbsp groundnut oil
   or vegetable oil
2 tbsp water
1 tsp shrimp paste or
   anchovy essence
3 skinless, boneless
   chicken breasts

To garnish:
One-half of a cucumber

What you do

1 **Peel** and **chop** the onion and garlic. Crush or chop the nuts.

2 Cut the root off the lemongrass, peel off the outside layer, and chop the middle section.

3 Put the chili pepper powder, coriander, cumin, cloves, cinnamon, nutmeg, and turmeric into a bowl.

(!) 4 Heat the oil in a wok or saucepan over a medium heat. **Fry** the onion for 3 minutes. Add the garlic and cook for 1 minute.

5 Add the lemongrass and spices, and cook for 30 seconds. Spoon the mixture into a blender.

6 Add the shrimp paste and 2 tbsp water, and **blend** to a smooth paste.

7 On a board, cut the chicken into ½-in. (1-cm) pieces. Put them into a bowl.

8 Stir the blended mixture into the chicken. **Cover** and **chill** for 2 hours.

9 Soak 8 wooden **skewers** in cold water for 30 minutes.

10 Meanwhile, cut the cucumber into ½-in. (1-cm) slices, then cut them into quarters.

⊘ 11 Push the chicken pieces onto the skewers.

⊘ 12 **Preheat** a grill to medium hot. **Grill** the *satay* for 5–7 minutes, turning them over halfway through. Serve with Peanut Sauce (page 12), garnished with cucumber quarters.

Aromatic Chicken

In Indonesia, this dish is often prepared for a feast or special occasion. It tastes even better if you **chill** it overnight—but let it cool before you put it into the refrigerator. **Reheat** it in a saucepan until it is piping hot, before serving with basmati or fragrant Thai rice.

What you need

1 tbsp **ground** coriander
1 tsp ground cumin
½ tsp ground cloves
½ tsp ground nutmeg
½ tsp ground turmeric
1 onion
1-in (2½-cm) piece fresh ginger
1 chicken stock cube
1 cup (240 ml) water
8 boneless chicken thighs or 4 chicken breasts cut in half
1 tbsp groundnut oil or vegetable oil

To garnish:
Crispy onion rings (page 25)

What you do

(!) 1 **Dry-fry** the spices in a frying pan for 30 seconds. Pour the spices into a blender.

2 **Peel** and roughly **chop** the onion and the ginger. Add them to the blender, and **blend** until smooth.

3 Crumble the stock cube into the blender. Add half the water and blend again.

4 Pour the spice mixture over the chicken in a bowl. **Cover** the bowl with plastic wrap and chill for 2 hours.

(!) **5** Heat the oil in a saucepan over medium heat. Using **tongs**, lift the chicken pieces into the pan, and **fry** for 2–3 minutes on each side. Add the rest of the water and spice mixture in the bowl, and stir well.

6 Cook over medium heat until **boiling**. **Cover** and **simmer** for 50 minutes.

7 Serve hot with rice and crispy onion rings (see box).

CRISPY ONION RINGS

Crispy onion rings are used to garnish many Indonesian dishes. Indonesians use shallot-like onions, but you can use ordinary onions. You need:

1 onion
2 tbsp groundnut or vegetable oil

1. Peel and **slice** the onion thinly.

(!) **2.** Heat 2 tbsp oil in a frying pan. Fry the onion rings over a medium heat for 5 minutes, until crispy. Lift onto a paper towel, then serve.

Spiced Beef and Coconut Stew

This recipe uses beef, but traditionally it is made with buffalo meat. If you cannot buy the root galangal, use fresh ginger and lemon juice for a similar flavor.

What you need

1 onion
2 cloves garlic
1-in. (2½-cm) piece fresh galangal or 1-in. (2½-cm) piece fresh ginger and 2 tbsp lemon juice
1-in. (2½-cm) piece fresh ginger
1–2 red chili peppers (optional)
1 stem lemongrass
½ tsp ground turmeric
½ tsp ground coriander
½ tsp ground cumin
1 lb (500 g) braising steak
1 lime leaf (optional)
1 tsp ready-prepared tamarind paste or dash lemon juice
14 oz (400 ml) can coconut milk
½ cup (100 ml) water
2 tbsp groundnut or vegetable oil
6 new potatoes

To garnish:
Crispy onion rings (page 25)

What you do

1 **Peel** and roughly **chop** the onion and garlic. Peel and **slice** the galangal and ginger.

2 Cut the chili peppers in half and throw away the seeds. **Chop** the chili peppers finely, washing your hands thoroughly afterwards.

3 Cut the root off the lemongrass. Peel off the tough outer layer. Chop the middle section finely.

4 Put the onion, garlic, galangal, ginger, lemongrass, chili pepper, turmeric, coriander, and cumin into a blender and **blend** until smooth.

5 Trim fat from the beef. Cut into 1-in. (2½-cm) cubes. Mix the beef and spice paste together in a bowl.

6 Tear the lime leaf (if using) into 4 pieces. Add them to the beef, **cover** the bowl with plastic wrap, and **chill** for 2 hours.

7 Put the tamarind paste into a bowl. Stir in the coconut milk and ½ cup (100 ml) water.

⚠ 8 Heat the oil in a wok, and **fry** the meat over high heat for 3 minutes.

9 Stir in the coconut milk mixture and bring to a **boil**. Cover and **simmer** for 1½ hours.

10 Wash the potatoes and add them to the pan. Cook for 20 minutes.

11 Serve with basmati or fragrant Thai rice, garnished with crispy onion rings (page 25).

Steamed Cabbage with Coconut

In Indonesia, cooks **steam** food in a bamboo steamer resting over a wok full of **boiling** water. This is very healthy, because it uses no fat. If you do not have a steamer, rest a metal colander over a pan of boiling water.

What you need

White flesh of half a coconut

14 oz (400 g) white cabbage or 1 large head Chinese leaf

½ of a red chili pepper (if you like it)

2 cloves garlic

1 lime

1 tsp palm sugar or brown sugar

2 tsp shrimp paste or anchovy essence

What you do

(!) 1 Wrap the coconut in a dish towel and put it on the floor outside. Tap the coconut with a hammer until it cracks, then pull it apart. Let the clear fluid **drain** away, and cut off the hard brown shell.

2 Using a grater, **grate** half the flesh from inside the coconut.

3 If using white cabbage, cut it into quarters. Cut out the hard stem and throw it away. **Shred** the cabbage. If using Chinese leaf, cut off the base and shred the leaves.

4 Cut the chili pepper in half and throw away the seeds. **Chop** the chili pepper finely, washing your hands thoroughly afterwards.

5 **Peel** and crush, or chop, the garlic. Using a lemon squeezer, squeeze the juice from the lime.

6 Bring a large pan of water to a boil.

(!)7 **Toss** the cabbage or Chinese leaf and pepper together in a bowl. Put them into a steamer. **Cover** the steamer and place it carefully over the pan of boiling water. Steam for 3 minutes for slightly crunchy vegetables, or longer, if you prefer.

8 Mix the coconut, garlic, lime juice, sugar, and shrimp paste together. Put the cabbage into a serving bowl and spoon over the coconut mixture. Toss well and serve.

Carrot and Mooli Salad

In Indonesia, people often serve salads of **grated** vegetables at the same time as other dishes. Their cool, fresh flavors go well with spicier foods. Many grocery stores sell mooli, which is also called white radish. It has a slightly peppery taste.

What you need

5 medium carrots
9 oz (250 g) mooli

*For the **dressing**:*
3 tbsp white wine vinegar
1 tbsp superfine granulated sugar
½ tsp salt
½ of a red chili pepper (if you like it)
½ of a green chili pepper (if you like it)
3 tbsp water

What you do

1 **Peel** the carrots and the mooli. Cut off both ends. **Chop** the vegetables into pieces about 2 in. (5 cm) long.

2 Cut a thin slice off the side of each piece, so that it lies flat on a chopping board.

3 Cut each piece lengthwise into thin slices, then cut the slices the other way to make matchstick-shaped pieces. Put the pieces into a bowl.

4 Cut the red and green chili peppers in half, and throw away the seeds. Chop the chili peppers finely, washing your hands well afterwards.

5 Stir the vinegar, 3 tbsp water, sugar, and salt together until the sugar has **dissolved**. Add the chili peppers, if using.

6 Pour the dressing over the carrot and mooli. **Toss** well, and spoon onto a plate before serving.

ANOTHER VERSION

If you cannot find mooli, you could replace it with the following amounts of bean sprouts or apples:

6 oz (170 g) bean sprouts or 4 large eating apples

1. Rinse the bean sprouts with cold water and pat them dry, or peel and coarsely **grate** the apples.

2. Add to the other ingredients and toss in the dressing. Serve immediately.

Spicy Scrambled Eggs

This simple dish is popular all over Indonesia. People serve it as a snack, or as part of a main meal with other dishes. They add different vegetables, depending on what grows on their island. Either use the vegetables suggested here, or choose your own.

What you need

4 green onions
1-in. (2½-cm) piece
  fresh ginger
2 cloves garlic
1 carrot
2 oz (50 g) green
  beans
2 eggs
2 tbsp groundnut
  or vegetable oil
6-oz (170-g) can white
  crab meat
1 tbsp soy sauce
Pinch of chili pepper
  powder (if you
  like it)

What you do

1 Trim both ends from the green onions. Finely **slice** the white and the green parts, keeping them separate.

2 **Peel** and **grate** the ginger.

3 Peel and crush, or finely **chop**, the garlic.

4 Peel the carrot and cut off both ends. Cut it into pieces 2 in. (5 cm) long.

5 Cut a thin slice off each side of the carrot so that it lies flat on a chopping board.

6 Cut each piece lengthwise into thin slices, then cut the slices the other way, to make thin, matchstick-shaped pieces. Put them into a bowl.

7 Trim the ends off the beans and cut them in half.

8 Crack the eggs into a bowl, and **beat** them lightly with a fork.

(!) **9** Heat the oil in a wok over medium heat. **Stir-fry** the white part of the green onion for 1 minute. Add the ginger, garlic, carrot, and beans, and stir-fry for 3 minutes.

10 Add the crab meat, soy sauce, and green onion tops. Stir-fry for 1 minute.

11 Add the chili pepper powder and eggs. Stir-fry until the eggs have set. Serve hot.

Sumatran-Style Lamb Chops

Curry is very popular in Indonesia, where it is called *kare* (pronounced *car-RAY*). Cooks often make a large amount of curry at the beginning of the week, and serve it every day with different dishes. Curry recipes from the island of Sumatra are usually medium-hot, and are cooked with coconut milk.

What you need

1 small onion
2 cloves garlic
1-in. (2½-cm) piece fresh ginger
½ stem lemongrass
½ of a red chili pepper (if you like it)
4 candlenuts or Brazil nuts
½ tsp **ground** turmeric
Salt and pepper
2 tbsp groundnut or vegetable oil
4 lean lamb chops
2 tbsp lemon juice
1 tsp palm sugar or brown sugar
1 tsp ground coriander
1 cup (240 ml) coconut milk
1 cup (240 ml) water

What you do

1 **Peel** and finely **chop** the onion and garlic.

2 Peel and **grate** the ginger over a plate.

3 Cut the root off the lemongrass and peel off the tough outer layer. Chop the middle section finely.

4 Cut the chili pepper in half and throw away the seeds. Chop the chili pepper finely, washing your hands afterwards.

5 Put the onion, garlic, ginger, lemongrass, pepper, nuts, and turmeric into a blender. Add salt and pepper, and **blend** until smooth.

(!) 6 Heat the oil in a wok, and **fry** the spice mixture over medium heat for 3 minutes. Add the lamb chops. Fry for 2 minutes on each side, until they are brown.

7 Add the lemon juice, sugar, coriander, and 1 cup (240 ml) water. Stir well, **cover**, and **simmer** for 25 minutes.

8 Stir in the coconut milk, and simmer for 5 more minutes. Serve hot with Festive Rice Cones (pages 38–39) or rice noodles.

Tofu Omelettes

Indonesian cooks use chicken and duck eggs to make omelettes. Omelettes can be served as a snack, or rolled up and sliced as a **garnish** for other dishes (see page 39). This popular omelette recipe adds onion, chili pepper, and tofu to the eggs.

What you need

1 onion
½ of a red chili pepper (if you like it)
2 oz (50 g) tofu
4 eggs
2 tbsp water
Salt and pepper
2 tbsp groundnut or vegetable oil

To garnish:
Sprigs of cilantro

What you do

1 **Peel** the onion. Cut off the tip. Holding the root end, cut it into thin **slices.**

2 Cut the chili pepper in half and throw away the seeds. **Chop** the chili pepper finely, washing your hands thoroughly afterwards.

3 Cut the tofu into ½-in. (1-cm) cubes.

4 Crack the eggs into a bowl. Add 2 tbsp water and some salt and pepper, and **beat** lightly with a fork.

5 Stir in the onion, chili pepper, and tofu.

(!) **6** Heat 1 tbsp of the oil in an 8-in. (20-cm) non-stick frying pan over medium heat for 1 minute. Spoon half of the egg mixture into the pan.

7 Cook the mixture for 2–3 minutes, until the underside of the omelette is brown when lifted with a spatula.

8 Using a spatula, turn the omelette over and cook the other side.

9 Put onto a plate and repeat steps 5–8 to cook the second omelette. Serve garnished with cilantro.

FAST FOOD

On the Indonesian island of Madura, local people hold a series of races for bulls every year. Before the racing season starts in August, the bulls are fed beer, eggs, and chili peppers. This diet is said to make them run faster.

Festive Rice Cone

This dish is often served at Indonesian festivals. The rice is made into a cone shape by being pressed into a cone-shaped sieve and then turned upside down on the plate. If you don't have a cone-shaped sieve, serve the rice on a plate in a mound shape.

What you need

1 clove garlic
1 onion
2 tbsp groundnut
    or vegetable oil
½ tsp ground
    turmeric
7 oz (200 g) basmati
    or fragrant Thai
    rice
1 cup (240 ml)
    coconut milk
1 stem lemongrass

*To **garnish***:
For omelette strips:
2 eggs
Salt and pepper
1 tbsp groundnut
    or vegetable oil
Half a cucumber

Crispy onion rings
    (page 25)

What you do

1 **Peel** and **chop**, or crush, the garlic.

(!) 2 Peel and **slice** the onion. Heat the oil in a medium saucepan and **fry** over medium heat for 2 minutes. Add the garlic and fry for 1 minute.

3 Add the turmeric and rice, and cook for 3 minutes, stirring all the time.

(!) 4 Stir in the coconut milk and 1¼ cups (300 ml) hot water, and bring to a **boil**.

5 Hit the lemongrass with a rolling pin, or bend it a few times to release its flavor. Add it to the rice and **simmer** for 15 minutes, until the liquid has been soaked up. (Add water if the rice sticks.)

6 Crack the eggs into a bowl, and add salt and pepper.

(!) 7 Heat the oil in a frying pan. Pour in half the egg mixture and cook for 2–3 minutes, until the underside of the omelette is brown. Using a spatula, turn the omelette over and cook the other side. Lift the omelette onto a board to cool. Repeat to make a second omelette.

8 Roll the omelettes up and cut them into 1-in. (2½-cm) slices.

9 Cut the cucumber into thick slices, then cut each slice into quarters.

10 Lift out the lemongrass. Put a cone-shaped sieve into a bowl and spoon the rice into the sieve, pressing down firmly.

11 Pour the rice onto a plate and garnish with omelette strips, crispy onion rings (page 25), and cucumber.

Coconut Pancakes

Indonesian meals usually finish with fresh fruit, such as bananas or paw paws (papayas). People serve desserts like the one in this recipe on special occasions. Indonesian desserts can be very sweet— traditionally, this recipe has double the amount of sugar suggested here.

What you need

For the filling:
5 tbsp dark brown sugar
¾ cup (75 ml) water
4 oz (100 g) **desiccated** coconut

For the pancakes:
4 oz (100 g) plain flour
1 egg
1¼ cups (300 ml) milk
3 tbsp groundnut oil or vegetable oil

To garnish:
Small piece of fresh coconut

What you do

1 Put the sugar and ¾ cup (75 ml) water into a non-stick saucepan. Heat over low heat until the sugar has **dissolved.**

2 Add the coconut and cook for 3 minutes, until the coconut has soaked up the liquid. Turn the heat off and leave to cool. Turn the oven on to its lowest setting.

3 Put the flour, egg, and milk into a blender, and **blend** into a smooth batter.

(!)4 Heat 1 tbsp of oil in an 8-in. (20-cm) non-stick frying pan over medium heat. Add 2 tbsp pancake batter. Tilt the pan to cover the base.

5 Cook for 2 minutes, or until the surface of the batter has set.

6 Using a spatula, turn the pancake over and cook for 2 minutes.

7 Slide the pancake onto a heatproof plate. Cover it with foil and keep it in the oven. Repeat steps 4–6 to make 8 pancakes.

8 Put a spoonful of coconut filling into the middle of each pancake. Roll up the pancakes.

9 Using a vegetable peeler, shave off some slices of fresh coconut and scatter them over the pancakes. Serve immediately.

Fruit Salad

Many different types of fruit grow on the islands of Indonesia. This dish is a simple fruit salad that might traditionally be served after a meal. It includes a pomelo, but if you cannot find one, try using a grapefruit for a similar flavor.

What you need

1 pineapple
1 mango
1 pomelo
2 bananas

What you do

1 Cut off the top and base off the pineapple. Stand the pineapple on a chopping board on one end.

2 Starting from the top, carefully cut large strips of the skin away from the pineapple flesh. Throw away the skin.

3 Cut the pineapple in half and then cut each half again lengthwise. Cut off the tough core in the middle of each piece and throw it away. Cut the pineapple flesh into bite-sized pieces.

4 Cut the mango lengthwise into three equal pieces. The middle piece will contain the flat stone. **Slice** the fruit flesh into long strips from around the stone and cut off the skin.

5 **Peel** the thick skin off the pomelo. Cut the fruit into slices.

6 Peel and cut the bananas into slices.

7 Arrange the fruit on a large plate and serve.

COCONUTS

Coconut is an important ingredient in Indonesian cooking, but coconuts can be used in many other ways. Coconut flesh can be dried and crushed to produce coconut oil. A fiber called coir, made from the husk of the coconut, is used to make carpets, matting, and thatching for roofs. The shell of a coconut makes excellent charcoal, too.

Further Information

Here are some places to find out more about Indonesia and Indonesian cooking.

Cookbooks

Braman, Arlette N. *Kids Around the World Cook!* New York: John Wiley & Sons, 2000.

Cook, Deanna F. *The Kids' Multicultural Cookbook.* Charlotte, Vt.: Williamson Publishing, 1995.

Pratt, Dianne. *Hey Kids, You're Cookin' Now.* Chattanooga, Tenn.: Harvest Hill Press, 1998.

Vezza, Diane Simone. *Passport on a Plate.* New York: Simon & Schuster, 1997.

Books About Indonesia

Arnott, Susi. *Indonesia.* Chicago: Heinemann Library, 1997.

Martin, Fred. *Next Stop: Indonesia.* Chicago: Heinemann Library, 1999.

Measurements and Conversions

3 teaspoons=1 tablespoon	1 tablespoon=½ fluid ounce	1 teaspoon=5 milliliters
4 tablespoons=¼ cup	1 cup=8 fluid ounces	1 tablespoon=15 milliliters
5 tablespoons=⅓ cup	1 cup=½ pint	1 cup=240 milliliters
8 tablespoons=½ cup	2 cups=1 pint	1 quart=1 liter
10 tablespoons=⅔ cup	4 cups=1 quart	1 ounce=28 grams
12 tablespoons=¾ cup	2 pints=1 quart	1 pound=454 grams
16 tablespoons=1 cup	4 quarts=1 gallon	

Healthy Eating

This diagram shows which foods you should eat to stay healthy. Most of your food should come from the bottom of the food pyramid. Eat some of the foods from the middle every day. Only eat a little of the foods from the top.

Healthy eating, Indonesian-style

Indonesian cooking uses a lot of foods that belong in the bottom half of this pyramid. Many dishes blend lightly cooked vegetables with lean meat, such as chicken and fish. Food is often **stir-fried** in a small amount of oil, or cooked in a spicy sauce. Rice is a vital part of most Indonesian meals, because it grows so plentifully. It is served with most dishes, or sweetened with lots of sugar as a dessert.

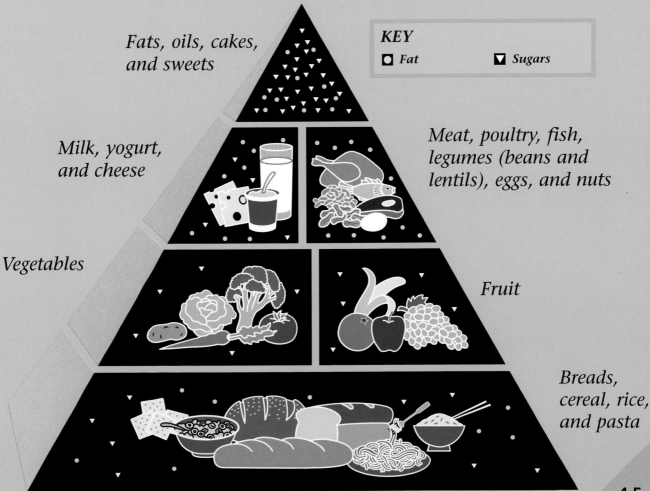

Fats, oils, cakes, and sweets

KEY
◻ Fat   ▽ Sugars

Milk, yogurt, and cheese

Meat, poultry, fish, legumes (beans and lentils), eggs, and nuts

Vegetables

Fruit

Breads, cereal, rice, and pasta

Glossary

archipelago line, or chain, of islands

beat mix ingredients, using a fork or whisk

blend mix ingredients together in a blender or food processor

boil cook a liquid on the stove. Boiling liquid bubbles and steams.

chill put a dish into the refrigerator for a while before serving

chop cut into small pieces using a sharp knife

cover put a lid on a pan, or put foil or plastic wrap over a dish

desiccated in this book, dried, flaked coconut flesh

dissolve mix something into a liquid until it disappears

drain remove liquid, usually by pouring something into a colander or sieve

dressing sauce for a salad

dry-fry cook at a high heat without any oil

fry cook something in oil in a pan

garnish decorate food, for example, with fresh herbs

grate break something, such as cheese, into small pieces using a grater

grill cook on an outdoor grill

ground made into a fine powder

marinated soaked in sauce before cooking

monsoon wind that blows across an area, often bringing heavy rainfall

peel remove the skin of a fruit or vegetable

plantation very large farm that usually only grows one crop

preheat turn on the oven in advance, so that it is hot when you are ready to use it

reheat heat food thoroughly again

roast cook in a hot oven

shred cut or tear something into small pieces

simmer cook liquid on the stove. Simmering liquid bubbles and steams gently.

skewer long wooden stick for holding food

slice cut ingredients into thin, flat pieces

steam cook in hot steam from boiling water

stir-fry cook foods in a little oil over high heat, stirring all of the time

tongs u-shaped kitchen utensil used for turning over hot food

toss mix ingredients, for example, in a salad

Index